Brother David
A Long Journey Home

JOHN PEARSON

*Best Wishes
Malcolm & Jackie
15/12/16*

Copyright © 2015 John Pearson

All rights reserved.

Cover design by J Pearson

Book design by J Pearson

No part of this book can be reproduced in any form or by written, electronic or mechanical, including photocopying, recording, or by any information retrieval system without written permission in writing by the author.

Published by J Pearson

Printed by Book Printing UK www.bookprintinguk.com
Remus House, Coltsfoot Drive, Peterborough, PE2 9BF

Printed in Great Britain

Although every precaution has been taken in the preparation of this book, the publisher and author assume no responsibility for errors or omissions. Neither is any liability assumed for damages resulting from the use of information contained herein.

ISBN 978-1-5186-7714-4

DEDICATION

To Mum and Dad and the telling of old stories.

CONTENTS

	Preface	i
1	Finding a Path	1
2	Between Sleep and Awake	8
3	A Caravan Pilgrim	14
4	Becoming Visible	18
5	The Wishing Stone	24
6	Past, Present and Future	30
7	Ambrose	36
8	Being the Same but Different	40
9	Learning a little Magic	44
10	A Skylark and a Squirrel	48
11	Every inch a Bridge	52
12	Epilogue	56

PREFACE

The story of Brother David: about his thoughts and dreams, people and places around him, existing both in the now and the past.

A Franciscan friar, David is content in his life but continually searching for something unknown – as if he were attempting to make a jigsaw without having the picture to show the finished image, and not knowing whether the piece he is picking up fits his jigsaw or someone else's.

Set in North Yorkshire, the friary has many comings and goings, and David is very much part of this. He loves to wander, in the woods and moors – but also in his thoughts. A chance meeting and a string of curious events sparked David's imagination and this searching journey seemed to run parallel to his own, at times more than overlapping and also challenging his beliefs.

This is a story, although some of the place names are familiar and the characters are more typical than real. We are all on a long journey home and although some of this journey must be on our own, others have often been there before us.

1 FINDING A PATH

"Hello David!" The voice came from down the street; it was market day and fairly busy. "It is David?" I turned and looked. The voice was familiar but I couldn't place the face. I must have looked puzzled because he said, "You don't remember me, do you?"

It must have been my brain not working because I'd just had new glasses, so there was obviously nothing wrong with my sight. It was just that the faces belonging to the bank of people I have known gets muddled. "No, no, it's my fault. I am sure you're right. Yes, I am David." Oh dear, that didn't sound right, or particularly welcoming. I tried again. "Well, David Lyth actually. Hello. Please forgive me. How do you do?" This poor man was probably wishing he had never called me, but I caught sight of a smile as he said, "Brother David." I still had no idea who he was and I really don't do this social chat thing very well.

"You led a retreat two years ago on Holy Island. I was part of the men's group and helped with evening prayer," he went on, hoping for some glimmer of recognition behind my glasses. Ah yes, it did come back to me – like plugging a memory stick into a computer, the whole weekend suddenly flashed by – the tides, the birds, the good weather, walks by the shore, that amazing half-hour of silence during evening prayer.

"Rick! Yes, of course! It was such a good weekend, wasn't it? How have you been? What are you doing in this part of the world?" There I went, two questions at once and not even checking to confirm if his name really was Rick. "I'm so sorry. Please, would you like a coffee?" I stammered. I do that sometimes when I am nervous.

"Yes, that sounds great. I'm up here on business and decided to stay a couple of extra days." We walked towards the centre of town. I knew a nice little café just up from the bookshop. Morton is a small market town typical to North Yorkshire and located between the moors and the sea. It seemed to have escaped the building development that had changed so much of our area, probably because of the "big house" at the end of the town owning most of the land.

We went for coffee at Ida's Tearoom. We had little past to share – apart from this one weekend at Holy Island – and I would not have recognised him if I passed him in the street. We didn't seem to have very much in common, yet here I was inviting him for a coffee – and there were so many things waiting to be done today. This was an unscheduled stop, but the kind of thing that happened quite a lot to me. Others manage a polite, 'How are you?' and carry on with the rest of their day.

"Well here we are. What can I get you?" The café was busy but we managed to find a seat in the window. The background music was a saxophone and the smell of freshly ground coffee took me back to a time in Rome. In contrast, just outside the thin pane of glass people were rushing back and forth, carrying their goods. I decided to enjoy the coffee and the conversation.

Rick was easy to talk to and happy to lead the conversation, which suited me. I must say he had led an interesting life. I felt a little like the poor relation when I compared my world travels to his; I don't think there was a country Rick hadn't passed through at some time. I was particularly fascinated by his trek through Syria, following the old trade route. This was a different man to the one I met on the island; he was much quieter then, often slipping off for a walk. For this man there was a time for quiet reflection, a time for action and this time of sharing.

I would guess he was in his early sixties, a bachelor and from what I remember, a successful sales executive. I love to travel, he said, to follow the old paths and listen to the stories. I'm not interested in archaeology, that's just old bones. I'm more interested in discovering the people and what they did.

We enjoyed the coffee and talked more, my ears pricking up when he mentioned the Stylites. These were not those things that grow in caves. Stylites were men who chose the ascetic life, spending between 15 and 40 years at the top of a stone pillar; a life of prayer and contemplation, their solitude broken by pilgrims asking for prayer and healing. This was something I'd heard of and I felt a renewed quickening of interest. I could feel myself already drawn to the library.

As our time of coffee and biscuits was coming to a close, I felt somewhat awkward. I was unsure what to do next. Should I invite Rick back to the friary? This meeting was quite by chance but I felt it was significant. I felt a curiosity and wanted to know more, but at the same time my day was set out and I had tasks to complete, and I was sure Rick would have plans of his own. My timing is never good – knowing when to leave social gatherings or how to excuse myself early.

"Well, Rick, where are you off to next?" I asked. He explained that apart from meeting up with a friend in Whitby that evening, the rest of the day was open. "You are most welcome to join us at the friary for tea if you like."

He seemed more than happy to come along and insisted on picking up the bill on the way out. Rick followed me in his car on the short journey back to the friary. I wondered why I was doing this – was it just my continual quest for stories and knowledge? I always seemed to be looking for something, not knowing what it was but thinking it would be clear when I found it. My collection of oddments, things found, had accumulated over the years and cropped up in conversations, which in themselves were looking for further links. And what of my to-do list?

The approach to the friary was down a small lane, passing an outer fence and turning into a driveway. The trees at the front provided shelter from the prevailing wind and a place to amble in clement weather.

I took Rick around the building, explaining how it originally used to be an old farmhouse owned by the church; how young families would start a farming life here and then eventually move on to their own farm. The church gave it over to our order of Franciscans about fifty years ago. Some alterations had been carried out over the years and the land continued to be let out to neighbouring farms. As friars we worked in the community and supported the local churches. We also got involved with young people – confirmation groups visiting the friary and such things. We tried to encourage church communities by providing resources, ideas and projects.

Through the garden, and at the back of the house, was the chapel, a converted cattle shed – rather appropriate, I always felt – and retaining the rustic form of beams and timber lintels. There was an assorted mixture of furniture, chairs and kneelers, collected over the years from different churches. I explained that often we would say office in the study, as it could get rather cold in the chapel.

We sat together for a while in silence, the sanctuary light flickering in the corner. Then left the chapel without speaking, the wind picking up as we headed indoors. Coming back through the garden I pointed out the greenhouse. Brother Cyril liked to potter around there, tending to the tomatoes and cucumbers. Cyril was getting on in years and often got confused, saying the strangest of things, but on the other hand he could come out with some pearls of wisdom. We used to joke that there was one speed with Brother Cyril – slow, but gets the job done.

We came back to the front of the house and I explained that this was a house of two halves. To the left of the main house was a latter addition, long and lower with upper windows in the roof. The front door had a habit of sticking, but today, with a slight lift of the handle it opened with ease.

"Welcome to our humble abode. Do come in." I closed the door and took Rick down the narrow passage past the reception room, which we used as an office, and on into the dining room. We liked to think of this as the centre of the house. Most things happened around this table – upon it was laid more than just our daily bread. I went through to the kitchen and put the kettle on, thinking we could take a cup of tea to the library. Rick seemed quite at home. "This must seem a big difference to some of the monasteries you've visited," I suggested.

"First, a place needs to be real, with real people, before it can be thought to be holy. Thank you for your hospitality," he replied. His choice of words was interesting and I wasn't quite sure what to say. "Let's go through to the library."

We walked back through the passage and up two steps to the older part of the house. We passed the laundry room, lounge and came then to the library. I headed for my chair by the north window, and before long we were lost in conversation. I was sorry that Brother Michael was not around to meet Rick, but secretly glad because Michael had a habit of taking over the conversation and I wanted to know as much as I could about Rick's travels, the things he had seen, the people he had met, his stories. Brother Cyril's room was just above the library and all was quiet – he was no doubt having an afternoon nap; he would often fall asleep reading a book.

I continued to probe about the Syrian Stylite or Pillar Saint, St Simeon the elder. Rick explained that around the year 423 Simeon took to a pillar and stayed there till his death 37 years later. The Stylites held to the belief that this form of self-crucifixion would ensure the salvation of their souls. I struggle to concentrate on one hour of contemplation or prayer at any one time! Did these folk really intend to never come down? To be tormented by demons and ministered to by angels is acceptable for story books but what about the physical body? Certainly, life was hard, but this was extreme. Were they really claiming that this was the way to salvation? This kind of journey was indeed solitary and the loneliness must have been crushing, but people came from great distances to offer their intentions and ask for healing. They must have had their food, and clothes provided and basic needs tended to.

Time moved on and the comfort of the library had to be left. Rick had an appointment at Whitby and the next day he was back to Oxfordshire. I also had some catching up to do. Brother Michael was away for a couple of days and it was down to me to prepare the evening meal. We said our goodbyes and the friary returned to its solitary status. In the quiet of that early evening, I took Brother Cyril a cup of tea and a ginger biscuit, with a promise of shepherd's pie later. He asked who our visitor had been and I recounted the stories of Syria and Simeon the Stylite. "Ah yes! He inspired Daniel, who took up the same occupation in Constantinople; feast day December 11. Crazy men. I'm blessed if I know why they did it. Shepherd's pie sounds good."

The rest of the evening seemed to pass slowly. Most of the office jobs were finished and the meal was indeed good. Brother Cyril rambled on about his Army days and I listened patiently for the umpteenth time. As we moved into evening office my quiet time was spent pondering on these extraordinary holy men who sat on pillars, and Rick's words that "being holy is about being real." These statements seemed to be so far removed from each other, but perhaps there was truth in both. I did yearn for the life of a hermit but I was sure it wouldn't suit me at all. I enjoyed my simple comforts and needed folk around me too much.

Tomorrow, I decided, I would dig a little further and find out more about these extreme men who sought such an austere life. I was well aware that I had been on this ground before. But if there was a path to be found here, I should at least explore the route.

# A LONG JOURNEY HOME

2 BETWEEN SLEEP AND AWAKE

The following weeks didn't turn out the way I expected as is often the way. A long line of plans and ideas were deferred, and sometimes lost. I knew I needed to build in some escape time. My head was becoming full of all manner of things and just like a filing tray, needed time to sift through the useful and the rubbish. The weather hadn't been good and I'd been unable to get out for walks. It had been a long winter, but spring was just around the corner and I sensed an awakening in the air.

The wind had dropped and the friary settled into stillness: the rattling of windows and doors, and whistling through gaps, that only seemed to be there when it blew in a certain direction ceased. This was not an immediate awareness. It was as if it had slowly dropped over a few days. In this quiet I took myself off to the library, and settled into my chair for what I imagined would be half an hour.

The light was stirring up the dust and particles were sparkling like tiny galaxies. I felt I should get up and do a little house work, but the old chair was holding me fast. I remember looking around at all the books and wondering where to start; travel, history or the saints. I took a long sigh and slowly became part of the old chair. We'd been friends for many years and both knew what was about to happen. My eyes squinted at the sunlight and within that same moment, they were tight shut.

The library faded away in the silence and left me with my thoughts. Images and colours surrounded me and this dream world began to string them together with the most unlikely of connections. I felt in control and that if I wanted to, I could wake at any moment. As the images dispersed I had a sense of arriving. The location was uninviting, a pile of rocks that could have been a ruined ancient building, and although I could see no clear entrance, I entered and descended through the rubble, down and into an enormous cavern the size of a cathedral. This was a strange experience, as here under the rubble there was light with no obvious source. I felt there were many people there but I couldn't see anyone. This would normally bring about a sense of uneasiness and anxiety but on the contrary, it was so peaceful I felt as if it was the perfect place to be. There was a magnificent centrepiece to this extraordinary place. Its sheer beauty took my breath away and I knew I was somewhere very special.

There was no sudden end to this dream. It didn't just fade away and there was nothing else to jump to. The vision faded, but not that I noticed, as the sense of awe filled me to bursting. I was being brought back to reality by approaching footsteps. Brother Cyril, the sound of his sandals on the wooden floor and a slight hesitation in the steps. I pulled myself up a little as the door opened. "Brother Cyril. I think I must have nodded off." I shouldn't have felt guilty – Cyril was often asleep in his chair, book in hand. I don't think he heard me because he just announced, "I tried to catch you earlier, you have some post. Oh, and I brought you a cup of coffee." He left the coffee and an envelope on the small table and headed back. "Thanks, very much." I was too late, he must have been part way down the hall. I reached for the coffee, I felt I was in need of something to revive me. I looked at the clock. Surely that couldn't be right? It was ten past two and had only been a couple of minutes after two when I sat down. I checked my watch and it agreed – ten past two. This puzzled me. I walked around the room sipping my coffee and looking for clues. I stepped through the sequence of events, remembering each one clearly. The dream was vivid and my senses were alert. The whole thing must have taken more than just five minutes. I don't like it when I can't explain something I know has just happened, I wanted to sit back down and immediately fall asleep to recapture the moment I'd just left.

BROTHER DAVID

That first day in the library was not yet done, for I would normally have dropped everything and reached for the envelope. I didn't often receive post just for me and this was clearly addressed for Brother David. It was handwritten and bore a foreign stamp. I know a number of Franciscans around the world. Most who write to me are in Italy but I didn't recognise the handwriting or the stamp. Opening it up, I skimmed to the back. It was Rick. I sat back into my chair, thinking it had been almost three months since I last saw him. Where on earth was he? I began to read.

Rick had joined a party of men and completed a trek through part of the Sinai desert. He'd spent nights under the stars with the Bedouin, and watched the sun rise from the summit of Mount Sinai. Our sun had been hidden, as dark clouds came in from the sea. I felt the temperature dip and sank a little deeper into the chair. Rick talked about the Bedouin, their way of life, the food, Nabateaan inscriptions and St Katharine's Monastery. I imagined just how awesome it would be to ascend Mount Sinai. Rick described the journey as a pilgrimage, one that had been made by many before him. Some three thousand steps cut into the rock, known as the steps of repentance; broken in stages with shops for refreshments, a welcome stop, but not what you would expect to find. Rick seemed to play down the sight of the sunrise which, I am sure, must have been tremendous. But the words he then wrote caught me by surprise. He said he felt he was three-and-a-half thousand years too late for Moses, he had missed Elijah by some two-and-a-half thousand years and it was as if God had long since gone, too.

This letter was completely out of the blue. I hadn't heard from Rick since our chance meeting. He was not the sort of person to send postcards, comments about the weather and wish you were here. This letter was packed with information that urged you to want to find out more. I was particularly interested in St Katharine's Monastery. Rick described how he was given access to their library and some of their ancient books. He admitted he couldn't read a single word, but the imprint it left on him was regarding the work and time that went into its creation and that it had lasted so long. I was already looking for my passport and wondering how I could get to this place. Rick was just so lucky. The letter dropped to my lap and I began to gaze around our library. There were books upon books, almost up to the ceiling, filing cabinets and an oval dining table; a three-and a two-seater settee. There were colourful books, but the overall theme was brown. So this was a big part of my world, a place where I worked, rested and wiled away the hours. I began to think just how impossible it would be for all of us to be in one place at one time. We journey together on different roads, some are familiar and others are not. If we could view this from a great distance, perhaps it would look like a multi-dimensional maze of solitary people travelling together. There seems to be an exchange of energy when travellers from different roads meet, increasing each other's momentum. A little like orbiting planets and moons.

The rhythm of the friary should ideally be at Brother Cyril speed – slow and steady, thoughtful and consistent. Brother Cyril could well be over 150 years old in his style and manner. He carried with him a way of life that was both transparent and reflected lives of many Franciscans before him. Cyril brought a sense of calm to what was often a chaotic household. At the opposite end of the spectrum was Brother Michael, organised and knowing everything about everything. Michael was the man when it came to reporting and accounting. He seemed to enjoy the importance and probably assumed more responsibility than he needed to. A taskmaster, Michael liked to get on with the job so he could move onto the next challenge. I, on the other hand, seemed to swing between the two of them, wanting to be more like Michael because that was what was expected, but my inner self yearned for the contemplative searching.

We three were a strange mix and one would expect there to be more friction and sparks than there were. I'm sure it was our routine of prayer, work, rest and study that held us together. Just like a team of horses can only work together when hitched and harnessed in formation, each one in their own place and driven by the man with the reins. The team of horses is content that everything is in its place and together they keep in step, whether they are pulling a plough or a carriage at speed.

Our daily office was also a rhythm. It may also be referred to as the 'Book of Hours'. It's the church's official book of prayer, recited at set hours of the day and night. In our community it was an individual responsibility to keep the hours of prayer. This was a practical consideration as we were not often at home during these hours. Morning and evening prayer was in the chapel and occurred every day at 6am and 7.30pm. Purists wouldn't approve of our adaptation. End of day prayer (Compline) was often around 9pm and shared together in the study, commonly on Friday and Sunday nights. There was a real settling of the mind and spirit before sleep. We had a structure as a basis of living that ordered our movement and thoughts, providing focus for the spirit and in meeting with others around us. I do wish I could motivate my physical fitness in a similar way, my working hours were more to do with sitting and the heaviest thing I lifted was a book. I'm sure I wouldn't have the stamina to trek through the Sinai or up any mountain for that matter. I once did the Lyke Wake Walk, some 42 miles across the North York Moors. I would have been in my late teens and seem to remember I was talked into it by a friend. If it was not for my friend's father pulling a muscle, I would have been in trouble myself. The father dropped out and passed some of his waterproof gear onto me; a storm blew up that night and the heavens opened, and it was left to the two of us to finish it. There was nobody at the last checkpoint, so we just had to keep on going to Ravenscar. The memory of the finish is still blurred, we were both so exhausted. Walkers behind us had to stop due to flooding; I heard some were air-lifted out too. Perhaps this put me off expeditions. Having not been much of an athlete or competitor in my schooldays, I enjoyed seeing others achieve but it didn't seem necessary for me to win. Rick, of course, is a competitor and probably wins often, whatever he does.

The day moved on. Brother Michael returned from a meeting at Leeds. Cyril and I had prepared the evening meal of fish, potatoes, vegetables and a nice white sauce. Michael was eager to hear how our day had gone. I kept it simple, as compared to Michael's day, ours was rather dull. Michael rolled up his sleeves and helped with the washing up, and before we knew where we were, it was time for the evening office. Time seemed to skip a beat and we were gathered in the study for Compline. I was ready for this.

The study was on the first floor. Part way up the stairs in the old building, we turned right through a door and into the study, which was in the newer part of the house. From the history of the house I believe this used to be the apple store. The windows had been put in later. I would try to imagine I could smell the apples as I sat there. The study had a different feel, one of Cyril's favourite haunts. The pictures on the wall mostly belonged to Cyril and consisted of landscapes in oils. The room was an oddment, as you might wonder why we needed a library and a study. The truth was simple – it was a room of collected furniture, file storage and some old rugs thrown on a wooden floor. The name "study" was mentioned one day that nobody remembers and just stuck. However, it is quite comfortable sitting in the eves with a single south-facing dormer window. We probably chose this room for Compline as it was not far to take the next step to bed. As we began prayer, cup of hot chocolate in hand, there seemed to be a silent sigh as the day unwound, allowing the happenings, thoughts and words to drop away. I prayed quietly for Rick, not knowing where in the world he may be, but asking God to keep him safe. It was only then that I realised I didn't have a return address.

End of prayer is silent, with the sign of the cross made before each of us leaves in silence to our beds. Both Cyril and Michael are on the first floor in the old building. I leave by the second door in the study, remaining in the eves in the new part. My room also has the same type of dormer window. There is a spare bedroom next to mine, followed by the bathroom at the end of the corridor and the back stairs down towards the dining room, kitchen and back door. The wind sometimes whistles up these stairs in the winter. I had a feeling that sleep was not going to come quickly, despite the hot chocolate and Compline.

My dream returned a number of times over the next few months, but I was entering the building now from street level, still reaching the centrepiece and with the same strange mixture of peace and excitement. I decided to make some plans – vague plans, but plans nevertheless. An expedition of sorts. Discovery – on the moors and through the woods. The dream from the library came back to me and I wanted to return to that place. I also knew exercise would be good for me, and I did enjoy walking. I felt my eyes begin to close and resolved to create some time in the woods and on the moors.

3 A CARAVAN PILGRIM

The day seemed to have passed so slowly, I recall every striking of the clock, and it felt as if my whole body were responding to the slow tick-tock. Only the endless cups of coffee kept me from falling asleep. My trips to and from the kitchen should have told me, I had little interest in the work I was doing.

Things became lighter during evening meal, as conversation swung towards a recent quoits match. Cyril loved to sit and watch the game and was familiar with all the terms: Frenchman, Gater, Ringer. He was commenting on the new up and coming players, "these young lads are keen" he said. Fathers and grandfathers would hand down the secrets of their throw and how to outwit their opponents. Competition between the villages was strong, but so too were the friendships; and afterwards, a glass of ale.

In lots of ways it was the sort of evening to be inside, as the wind was whistling through the trees. However, I had been inside long enough, and so told the brothers I was going to see Aunty who lived on the village green. It was suggested I took the car but I declined, saying I needed the walk. It certainly was windy as I approached Mill Hill, the wind was blowing my garments so much I had to gather them tightly round me. Ugthorpe is a small village, and through time has changed little in size and ways. The lights in the houses on the green were inviting as I approached

Auntie's house. I gave one sharp knock on the door and called "Aunty, its Brother David" as I walked in. Before long we were sat by the fireside with a pot of tea and some homemade ginger biscuits.

This lady in her late eighties is known to all around as Aunty, irrespective of relationship. She loves company and tells the old stories, which I find so interesting to listen to. The word pilgrimage cropped up in our conversation and a whole story enfolded, as Aunty began to tell me about the Caravan Pilgrim. She told me how she was just fifteen in 1934, when the great Portiuncula drove into the village. This really captured my imagination, as the word Portiuncula was familiar to me being a Franciscan. Portiuncula is a small place within Assisi and the little church of St Mary of the Angels (referred to as Portiuncula) it was rebuilt by St Francis, at the beginnings of the Franciscan order. My further research found that Peter Anson was a Tertiary of St Francis in 1927, so it was quite understandable that he might refer to his caravan as Portiuncula.

Aunty continued her story. The caravan was pulled by two horses, Jack and Bill. They were to park up at The Black Bull for five weeks before setting off on the rest of their journey. Peter Anson was an artist and commissioned by a Catholic newspaper, to sketch and write about churches en-route. Peter was accompanied by a farrier, Anthony Rowe from Brotton, only a stones throw from here. Anthony must have travelled to Slough, as they set off on this caravan pilgrimage from Datchet; with smudges on their foreheads, it was Ash Wednesday and February the fourteenth. Aunty went on to say that the reason for the long stay at Ugthorpe, was that they had to trade the old caravan for a much lighter one. It would not have been possible for the two horses to haul a wagon of that size up the hills to Scotland. The route was to take them to Fort William, and finish back here at Ugthorpe. The trade was done in Guisborough with a family of gypsies. There was such a buzz in the village as the new caravan was fitted out for the journey.

I was amazed at auntie's memory, clearly this encounter had left an impression; then she reached for two books. "I have oft done that same journey with Jack and Bill" she said, "we journey to return; hopefully not as we started". One of the books was written by Peter Anson, The Caravan Pilgrim, and the other, The Brown Caravan by Anthony Rowe; aunty loaned me both books. I left also with a bag of biscuits and a few scones, aunty must bake at least three times a week. The wind had dropped a little as I strode out along the footpath. Walking just beyond The Black Bull, the sound of horses spooked by the night alarmed me. It were as if they were just around the corner; where Jack and Bill would have been in 1934.

I imagined that year and what a big event it would have been for such a small village. I would have loved to have met Peter and wondered what Anthony had returned to. There is something very attractive about a journey of this sort. All you need is contained within the caravan, and there is just one purpose in the task ahead; life and its complexities are left behind. I felt I was walking with Peter, wanting to know more about the sense of journey. A pilgrimage, I thought was something specific, within a larger journey, and as aunty had said, returning hopefully not as we started.

Peter and Anthony must have met many people, they would be fleeting encounters with local folk as they passed through; very different from our normal ways. We are only with them for a short space of time, we offer what we can and leave on the best of terms. It really helps to have a focus, Peter's aim was to sketch and keep a journal. These were to be a weekly input to The Universe newspaper. The roads in those days would be very quiet and even the sight of a horse drawn caravan, regarded as unusual; time to write, in these quiet hours. Already I was sold on the thoughts of a pilgrimage, but knew it was not to be. In some ways I was trapped in the normality of life, not finding time to go to the high ground, where I could glimpse the road ahead.

The old Mill was in sight, its sails now gone, and a change of purpose for this landmark. Although not occupied, the Mill was now a dwelling place for folk who only visited a few times a year. I now had only downhill steps towards the grove of trees, in which nestled the friary; a faint smoke being blown from the chimney drew me on. I wondered what I had missed, what was waiting for me. Did I feel guilty about being away; no, it was important that evening to journey with aunty, Peter and the Portiuncula.

Hot chocolate and compline in the study had a different feel, and an urge to view from a hilltop, the road ahead. Later I slipped into my cosy bed and began to read The Brown Caravan, by Anthony Rowe. This was a different view, from one who was concerned with the practical aspects, and his beloved horses. I turned briefly to Peter's book and the Ugthorpe chapter; about the people he wrote: "The outward expression of their faith is as natural and spontaneous as that of a Breton peasant or Italian contadino". Sleep was approaching as I recalled another man Father Haydock, who, while at Ugthorpe completed a commentary for the new English version of the Catholic Bible, based on the Douay Vulgate translation; he also completed the new chapel. Father Haydock had managed to escape the French revolution as he was in training at Douay. All of this from such a small village; what more can be achieved?

4 BECOMING VISIBLE

We often have guests staying over at the friary and as the guest room is in my quarters, it falls on me to look after the room – to see to it that clean linen, towels and necessaries are set out and the room dusted. The comings and goings of our visitors, household responsibilities, duties and business, are written on a coloured glass wallboard using a marker pen. This is Michael's way of steering our ship, and each breakfast time it's updated. The captain's log, as I call it, lives on the wall just inside the kitchen door. Of course, not everything makes it onto this log, much to Michael's irritation. It was one such log entry that brought Michael and I to cross words. This was probably more due to the various pressures of the week than the uncompleted tasks. Some of the text was partially rubbed out and there were more items on the board than normal, but Michael was not listening to any of that and stuck firmly to, "The job's not being done". Michael is a bit like a schoolmaster and I felt as if I was in for detention and writing one hundred times, "I must follow instructions." I did what I always do in these situations – retreat. I knew Michael was partly right, but also that he could have handled it a lot better. I felt I could see all the angles, but they were not up for discussion. My next strategy was also typical of me. After Michael had left I set to and completed all the outstanding jobs and a few more besides. It gave me great pleasure to clean the captain's log.

That same day there was a loud knock at the back door. Very few people come to the back door, as the only access is from the fields behind, or around from the front. I answered the door to an old man with many layers of clothes and a big smile. "Hello Harry, how are you? Come on in." We went through to the kitchen and I put the kettle on. Harry had been a frequent visitor to the friary, always unexpected, although there did seem to be a rhythm to his visits. Harry, we would say, was a man of the road. He wouldn't ask for anything he wasn't willing to work for – by chopping wood, clearing weeds or carrying out small repair jobs. Over the years I have known him, Harry has let me into part of his world, the roads he has travelled and the scrapes he has been in.

Harry's typical greeting was not to shake your hand, but to take the stance of a boxer and, with his left fist guarding his chin, he would sway from left to right and throw a right towards your left shoulder. It could be off-putting on your first meeting, but this was just Harry. A one-time professional boxer, with the nose and eyes to match, this short, stocky old man still looked the part, despite his years. I don't think anyone quite knew Harry's true age, but when it came to finding things for him to do, I sometimes hesitated at some of the more physical tasks. Harry would object strongly in his deep voice, "I can do that." "The booze", as Harry would say, was his downfall. "But what can I do?" Often I would notice bruises and cuts where he had been mixed up in fights. I guessed that after drinking he forgot his age and the younger ones would kick back at his taunts.

Strong tea and two sugars. "So, how long will you be staying with us, Harry?" I asked. "Just the two nights if that's okay. I'm heading towards Holmfirth." This was one of his favourite parts of the country and probably about as far south as he would venture – to the north he would travel to Glasgow and Alexandria, his own Scotland. Harry would only let you into some parts of his life – life before the road was never mentioned. Early days, family and his decision to be constantly on the move was not spoken about. The road was his life and I would like to think Harry regarded us as family, but I don't think anyone got that close. Our natural instinct was to be concerned for him and we hoped that one day he would settle down in what we regarded as normality. The reality is that Harry will one day be found dead and possibly at the roadside. And I do believe Harry would not want it any other way.

BROTHER DAVID

The chapel was always Harry's guest room, with his sleeping roll on the floor and a mug of strong tea. He said he couldn't sleep in a bed and didn't like to be a bother. We would often chat for a while after evening office – religion was never discussed, but Harry was comfortable to sit through our prayer time and I'm sure we weren't the only spiritual house he frequented. It was on these occasions that Harry would talk of his journey and how he kept some of his belongings hidden around the country – winter clothes, shoes and items he couldn't carry with him. I struggled to understand his way of living, as I have all my belongings around me and would be devastated if anything went missing when I wasn't around. Harry had very little, and what he had was not that important to him – a very different view of life. No wonder he was poked fun at and rejected by many. There was no telling when Harry would turn up on your doorstep, and sometimes he left so early in the morning you wouldn't know he'd been – everything would be left tidy, but his imprint was left on each one of us, and in different ways.

Harry and Rick, two very different people, but both on a journey with adventure, choosing directions and going with them, despite the opposing flow. I wondered just how many more people were travelling these extraordinary journeys. And dare I dream of travelling these roads? I was on a pretty uneventful path.

We were running short on milk and I opted to walk up to the village store, across the fields and down the lane. My path took me alongside the hedgerows and dry stone walls, where wind and weather had accumulated moss and debris. I wondered if this was Harry's route, out towards his beloved Holmfirth, and I realised I'd never seen Harry on the road – he just appeared at our door and disappeared again. At the time of Harry's walking, he might well be invisible – now that was something that would appeal to me, to walk for miles under a cover of invisibility. How could I conjure up such magic?

I had been pondering these things in my heart and mind now for some time – Rick and Harry, the community at the friary, travelling and adventure. Approaching sixty years of age, I recognised that most of my life had been dreaming about places out of reach and trying to find something I thought was lost. Decisions I'd made seemed to lead to familiar and well-trodden roads. I didn't regret any part of my life thus far and would continue these roads to the end. However, I was about to begin a number of short journeys that would unfold new beginnings and unearth lost treasures.

The sun was low in the sky and as I turned the corner I squinted at the light, which removed everything else from my vision. My natural defence was to shield my eyes with my hands, but it was too late – I tripped over an old root and down I went. As I fell, I heard someone shout, "Look out!" Everything went black, as I hit my head on a rock and fell into a place devoid of time.

Sounds began to break into this space – a skylark singing as he made his ascent – and I remembered the pain, my head throbbing. I felt I knew where I was and what had happened, but didn't want to move just yet, my eyes still closed. I could hear a voice as if in the distance saying, "Tha's been spared, tha's been spared; gently now, gently." There was a sense of a hand on my shoulder with a soft moving action. The voice became clearer and nearer, "Gently now." My eyes opened to a large figure, kneeling on the ground beside me, smiling and greeting me with reassuring words. I apologised and tried to sit up. "Tak thi time, I'm surprised thi didn't see this coming."

He looked familiar, but his dress was unusual. Farming attire, but not clothing I'd seen hereabouts. His dialect was local but again, not one I recognised. He asked where I was going and I could only say the friary. He looked at me puzzled and I pointed the way. "Ah, Hollins Farm," he said. I was too dazed to argue and he'd taken support of my arm – it was as if I was being carried like a sheep by the shepherd. We spoke as we walked, but I was not clear enough in my head to ask anything of this Samaritan. His words were soothing and amid my pain there was a sense of peace. The friary was within a short distance, sheep were bleating in the fields and the sun was beginning to fade from the sky. I paused for a moment, took a deep breath and in that same moment, realised I was quite alone. I turned quickly to see where my helper had gone, but the long path behind me was clear. This was silly, he couldn't just disappear! The fact of the matter was, he had. My motivation to reach home now was strong and so I pressed on.

I opened the back door and stepped into the kitchen. Brother Michael greeted me with, "Where have you been, so long?" and "Where is the milk?" It took him a couple of seconds, looking me up and down, before he said, "Good heavens! What happened to you?"

I began, "I seem to have had a little fall." A chair was provided and then more questions. "Oh, do be quiet, Michael. I will be all right". If nothing else, Michael was thorough, and we were soon off to the hospital for a full check-up. Nothing broken, only bruises and mild concussion. The best remedy, it seemed, was rest and pain killers. All the way back home, I was thinking about my Good Samaritan. Up to this point he'd not been mentioned. We stopped off at the supermarket to pick up the milk.

Back at the friary, Cyril had prepared some food – sausages, mash and onion gravy. I have to say, I enjoyed it very much; this was comfort food. During the meal it was Cyril's turn to catch up on the event and the story of my Samaritan came out. I went into detail about his strange clothing. Cyril suggested he might have been from the Moors' local history museum. Michael put it more simply – a hallucination caused by the bump on the head. "People do not just disappear." The dessert was a treacle pudding and custard. Cyril thought I needed something sweet, but I do know this was one of his favourites too. There was a long silence and then Cyril said, "It could have been an angel, in your time of need," and he went on to list a number of similar cases. If I didn't know Cyril better, I might have taken his comments as teasing, but he was serious and his description fitted. Michael, however, was not having any of this and brought the conversation to a close. "It's time David got some rest. I think an early night is in order." With that, we began to clear the table and wash the pots. I remembered the man had referred to the friary as Hollins Farm and asked Michael if he had ever heard of it being called this. He said not, but it should be easy enough to check in the library or in the old local books in our own library written by people from the moors and dales around the friary. We had over the years been given books, often when people died and families were clearing out houses. I told Michael I was going to sit in the library for a while before retiring, and he said he would check in on me later.

It was a little nippy in the library but it was where I wanted to be, so I put on my thick cardigan and snuggled into the old chair. The standard lamp cast a pool of light around me and the rest of the room faded into the distance. It was difficult to imagine life before the friary, but it really hadn't been that long ago. I was what is often called a late vocation, having first left school and worked in industry in the North East. I was in my late thirties when the call to the Franciscan way of life became a reality. But even as a boy, I had thought about becoming a priest, although I didn't make it as an altar boy. My father always said I could become an altar boy when I was big enough to reach the lectionary. Being slight of build (nicknamed "Shrimp") I never made it. I spent three years at a friary in Cornwall, followed by an attachment to a church in Manchester, then just over fifteen years ago, I moved to the friary. Cyril seemed like part of the building and Michael arrived just over ten years later. The bottom line though, is that amid the ups and downs, it felt right.

It had been a strange day and the Good Samaritan was playing on my mind. Was he real, or merely in my dream world? Cyril said he was probably an angel and my mind strayed into realms of belief and disbelief. For some strange reason I thought about the world being flat or round – people back in the 17th Century were at loggerheads about this and it became a question of belief, not only in the cosmic sense but also the religious. Looking at it from this century, it's impossible to imagine how people could be so fooled, as back in 300BC there was an idea that the earth was in fact a sphere, and this assumption was continued by many scholars thereafter. I had always been brought up to question things and decide my own mind, or at least to check out the source of the issue, rather than just to accept the opinions of others. This still didn't explain my helper, though it gave me a quiet determination not to let it go, and to dig a little deeper. His build and posture, as I recalled, was similar to that of a farmer, but his voice and gentleness implied knowledge of suffering. At about that point, Brother Michael came in to tell me he was off to bed, and that for the next week I was to rest.

5 THE WISHING STONE

I seemed to have slept long and deep that night. This may have been the tablets or the fact I just needed it. No recollection of dreams, just a sense of peace. Taking a week's rest seemed fraudulent and I began to wonder how best I could use the time.

After a light breakfast I returned to the library and began to browse the local history books. I had some knowledge of the area, but it was surprising how much more was unearthed that morning. We relate our surroundings to our own time scale and structures of how things are. To step back in time is difficult, even if we were in a museum. Our reference point is still the now. Dream world, imagination, fantasy, call it what you will, removes the reference temporarily or releases us from the need for one.

Imagination and creativity, seeing things far off and bringing it to reality through metaphors, has always been with me. Ingenuity is also part of me and has come out in the creation of resources for schools and churches. I am beginning to think Michael is right about my Samaritan, and that he resides in my immense imagination.

Among these local books I found one that was more about family history. But there, half way through, transcribed from parish records I made a discovery. Thomas Harland married Mary Wright of Hollins Farm

A LONG JOURNEY HOME

1656. A boundary between imagination and reality had just been crossed in the turning of a page. I was on the case and further research on the Internet revealed Mary was the only child of the Wright family and Hollins Farm was sold on the death of Elizabeth, widow of William, in 1682. My assumption was that the name of the farm changed with the new owners. This also dated my Samaritan to pre-1682, although name changes do take a long time to be accepted by local folk. I felt I wanted to share this discovery with the brothers, but decided to keep it within the boundaries of my new found land. Resisting the temptation to delve further, and curbing my imagination, I distracted myself with stories of pannier trails across the moors, caravans of ponies taking produce to and from Whitby. I felt the need to go for a long walk. It's strange how journeys begin without our knowledge, a direction emerges but we have no idea of the destination. A walk would clear my head. I thought of Rick and his adventures. This was an adventure with mystery, and I was part of this journey.

Leaving word as to my intentions for the afternoon, and packing a few items into a rucksack, I left the friary behind and set out across field and moorland. The air was clear and full of sounds and my step was brisk. I came to a stop as I heard the song of a skylark ascending. It was quite beautiful and I found myself listening as if for the first time. Skylarks are plentiful in these parts and I was familiar with their song. The last time I heard one was the day I fell. There is a determination about this small bird in its rising to the heavens, full of sweet notes that could only be as a loan to this earthly plain. I was totally captured by this transient bird, which seemed to have the ability to move between heaven and earth with ease. It was at this point I recalled the words of a hymn by Nicholas Postgate,

O sweetest Lord, lend me the wings
of faith and perfect love
that I may fly from earthly things
and mount to those above.

Father Postgate, of course was well known across the North York Moors. Born in Egton and brought up in the farming way, Nicholas left for Douai to train as a priest. He returned to his beloved moors hidden as a travelling farm worker and said mass in secret, as these were times of persecution for Catholics. It was one of my ancestors who Father Postgate was baptising when he was arrested and taken to York. There he died for his faith. It's very difficult to imagine Father Postgate's life, so intent on serving the Catholic community, but equally intent on avoiding capture. Safe houses would have markings known only to priests and a trusted few, hiding places and more doors than you would expect, for a swift exit. People who were caught with or thought to be helping priests were taxed heavily and often lost their land. These were strange times and I wondered whether we would do so much today, should it be necessary. I paused again, looked at my right and my left hand as if weighing the balance. How should it be?

I was approaching the river as it moved swiftly towards Whitby harbour, the railway line following its lead. The weather had been favourable, with just a light breeze, and the threat of rain had not come about. I began to pick up a different trail, a large paving of sandstone blocks that took me up through woodland. I had read of these earlier, pannier trails. This was steep and as I climbed, the sound of the river below faded. It was familiar territory, as I used to play here with two cousins who lived close by, our trousers so green from sliding down the bracken-covered Nab. As I walked on I would find the wishing stone. I remember beginning to think I had missed it, or that it had been moved or broken up. I was sure it was not as far into the woods as I had walked. It was a lot quieter, too. When I finally came upon the stone it was just as huge as I remembered (I know often things look smaller as we grow up). There was no-one around, so I just had to climb through the centre of the stone, a large crevice, and make a wish. We would never dare tell each other what we'd wished for, for fear of it not coming true. As a child I mustn't have wished for anything significant, or I would have remembered it coming true.

I walked on a little further and left the path to my right. Approaching an edge I heard the river below and my intake of breath was sharp as I realised just how high up I was. Deciding to rest for a while, I took out my flask and something to eat. There was a sense of timeless peace, right here where I was resting. It came over me slowly as my body leaned into the place where I'd sat. My breathing slowed and I became aware of many different sounds. Each bird had its own location and purpose and the sounds of the branches moving in the breeze provided the background frequency to this new concerto. The river roar was interspersed with flashes of crisp sounds as it collided with countless rocks. I felt my eyes beginning to close as my mind didn't want to be distracted by visual content. I don't recall how long I stayed at this place. It was a time in itself, seeming like an age, yet over too soon, a place on the edge, between one thing and another. I had experienced things before when in meditation, but that was usually in the quietness of the chapel. I wanted to know what was special about this place – or was it just about my thoughts that day? It was as if the volume control of my senses had been turned up high and I'd been drawn into the reality of my surroundings, almost like entering from another world. I knew I wanted more of this. Part of me would describe it as a drug, but like the skylark as it ascends vertically and descends in the same manner, it remains on the edge, holding balance.

There are more things that puzzle me than those that I understand, and often I know that I know not, but I choose to continue in my not knowing, rather than delve into the why of it all. These words seemed so important that I wrote them down. They seemed to be a doorway through which I could access change. My life to that day had been partly dictated by external influences, tradition, family expectations and my own choices to maintain favour. This door was not a radical, futuristic door, whose purpose was to transform the traveller into something alien. People seemed quite busy doing that sort of thing already. No, this door felt more like a mirror, having the properties to reflect the inner self. Now on the surface, that was a scary thought, but somehow it felt right. Life, I thought, had brought about these insights before in some guise or another, perhaps through books or something a wise friend had spoken about. It was not the time to take notice then, but there on that edge, it was different. The journey I had started, not realising, had just given me a glimpse of the route and though the destination was unclear, it seemed reassuring.

I couldn't help thinking, as I sat there, about my Good Samaritan. I recalled his voice and gentle nature and put aside any thoughts of whether he was fact or fiction. I was in a hollow, beside a steep drop to the river. This provided some shelter from the prevailing wind and secrecy from the trail some one hundred yards behind me. This hideaway was part nature and part construction, overgrown with trees and vegetation. It was still possible to imagine a shape with purpose. My imagination was taking off at great speed. Could this have been a priest hiding place? The attire of the one who came to my aid was that of a farmer, but not of this age. My nature has always been to pursue the extraordinary, the more unbelievable the better. It is as if I have to prove people wrong, to uncover things not considered by others. My journeys of discovery have been many and strange, mostly cut short by discouraging comments, both internal and external. How often I had thought that the ways of the past were so relevant for today, but had been distorted or lost through time as a result of different needs. Those who found the need to control or manipulate and had the power to make those changes. I felt a great movement in my chest as I thought about injustice, restricting growth, diverting energy that would naturally induce mankind in the true direction. We must respond to a reference, a true note, as given by a tuning fork, so that we instinctively know when something is out of tune.

Time was moving on in many dimensions and although I desperately wanted to stay longer, the light would fade and I was expected back at the friary. My brothers would be concerned if I were even a little late home. This was my first time at the edge, but was to become for me, my hermitage. Rick was on a journey of adventure through history and community. Mine was that of a peregrinator, wandering from place to place, travelling more through places than visiting them. More like Harry in fact.

The edge was to permeate my prayer life following that day. It seemed more part of the spiritual than the physical. Even in the stillness of the chapel I could feel the breeze on my cheek, a faint smell of foliage and the sound of water. This imprint had been strong and requested my attention. It held no questions nor demanded action. It was I who had the questions and wanted to follow its lead.

A LONG JOURNEY HOME

6 PAST, PRESENT AND FUTURE

The accident faded and life went on pretty much as usual. Little was said and I kept my thoughts to myself. I found myself more active than reflective, taking more exercise and occupying my time with friary business. My creative side increased as writings and ideas flowed. There was a sense of a new me around and I quite liked it. Imagine you are trying to walk through deep mud in wellington boots, then step out of the boots and onto firm ground and begin to run. We often know we are capable of much more but are held back, often by words in the past such as, "You can't do that," "You are stupid," "That won't work." Said often enough and they become beliefs, holding us back like waist-deep mud. The change in me had happened not by any form of magic and certainly not by the bump on the head. A series of powerful images, sounds, emotions and memories through my heritage had pulled on everything that is precious to me, shifted my thinking, altered my perspective and enabled change in me at a level that I wouldn't find in books.

Many years ago I attended a convention with the Diocese of Nottingham. I had a keen interest in youth work and signed up to a couple of workshops in this field. The priest who led the group clearly wanted participation not just a passive bunch of what he would probably regard as time-wasters. He challenged the group and even held us back at the end, pushing for someone to take responsibility for the next session. If we were to be youth leaders, we should display some leadership. I can see that now, but then it was all so confusing, mixed with feelings of what should happen and, "Should I step forward?" I didn't. That night I retired early to my room with the intention of writing up some notes. This was difficult as my head was in a spin and I didn't know how to stop it. My last resort was prayer, and I must have fallen asleep sitting up in bed.

The next morning I met with a friend at breakfast. He was not with my group and so we exchanged uncomplicated thoughts on the previous day. As he spoke, the remnants of a dream began to emerge. This must have been visible, as my friend asked what was going on. "Oh it was just a dream I had last night" but as I began, the whole dream unfolded.

I was in my family house and noticed that upstairs, the walls were cracked and daylight could be seen through them. I began to panic and cleared everyone out of the house, as the damage was so severe, I thought the whole building might collapse. Once everyone was safe, and not knowing what to do, we set off to find friends who could help. The journey was long and part way through we were chased by a black dog, although a chain held him out of our range. Finding friends was a good feeling and describing what was happening was emotional. Our friends said we had to find the Master Builder, who would know what to do, and so off we went. The Master Builder seemed to be having a party and it didn't seem right to disturb him, but in no time at all he was there with us surveying the house. After a while he stroked his chin and said, "It'll all have to come down and re-build from the ground up, but the foundations are good."

It's funny but I really don't remember anything about the other workshops that weekend. But over those next few days, I pondered the dream and saw how closely it fitted my life up to that point. The walls that had been built, a good structure, had reached a point where they could no longer be fit for purpose. Major change was imminent, but the foundations were sound. New shapes and dimensions began to emerge and I took time to listen and to see this drawing become a dwelling place.

Today as I am writing this book, is another place, and there may still be time for more building. Mostly, additions arrive unnoticed, and we make more fuss about décor than function. Still, back to life then at the friary.

Morning breaks in a variety of ways and we assume just because the sun is shining, that it's going to be a good day. Quite the opposite, in fact, strong winds and rain were blowing in from the north. The house had different sounds, depending on the wind direction and I reached for my long coat. An umbrella would be useless today. My morning task was to drive to Whitby Railway Station some eight miles away to collect Brother Timothy.

Brother Timothy was a young man who was to spend a few months with us. There was no background given or directions, just to keep him busy before he was to move to Los Angeles. Arriving at the station, I opted to wait in the car till I could hear the train arriving. As the doors opened, folk began to rush to the local shops. It was market day and the small town was buzzing, despite the weather. A tall, dark figure struggled out of the train with bags and a guitar case. Recognising the habit, I ran across to help. The habit itself had seen better days. He had long straggly hair and a beard, but why did he not have a suitcase? There were more carrier bags than one person could manage, but it seemed someone else was already helping his disembarkment.

I greeted him and somehow we managed to get his belongings from the platform to the boot of the car. I wondered if he intended travelling to Los Angeles in the same way, and to be honest, looking at him, I would guess that would be a yes. I had to remind him to buckle up his seat belt and he launched into telling me all about his train journey. His account centred around encounters with fellow travellers, conversations that I wondered how he had got into, they seemed so unlikely; my very few train journeys, are solitary and uneventful. The only piece of personal information I gained was that he preferred to be called Tim. With all his talk there was no wonder nobody knew much about him, you couldn't get a word in edge ways to ask anything. There was no change in the weather as we arrived, and the stream of carrier bags flowed into the friary and rested in the hall.

Tim settled in immediately, finding a comfortable spot in the kitchen while Brother Cyril was fussing round preparing coffee and cake. Michael was the one to quiz Tim and over coffee managed to piece the story together. I had already built up my own picture of this strange person – very untidy, unorganised and working to a set of values that could not practically fit into this world. He came into our quietness like the gale that was blowing outside. As Franciscans, we are expected to care for the stranger at the door, be accepting and tolerant, not to make judgements and to offer all that is needed. Was this to extend to our brother? I desperately wanted to show Tim to his room and shift all his bags there too. He seemed too intent on listening to Cyril and Michael. I let him know that I would show him to his room when he was ready and that I would be in the library. "Oh, you have a library? I'll join you," he said.

We must have sat for nearly an hour and within our conversation I shared some of my journey, parts I would not normally talk about. I noticed his eyes, sharp like a bird of prey, interpreting my words and coaxing further. His face beneath the beard seemed long and drawn, I knew his age to be just over thirty, but he looked at least ten years older. He had spent time in Bangalore, India, and asked if I had ever been to India. My travels had been confined to parts of the Mediterranean, with no real desire to venture further. Tim paced the library, picking up books, flicking pages and putting them carefully back on the shelves. He had an interest in most things that centred around people. Larger than life in many ways, Tim was the type of person you would not forget quickly, I wanted to ask about Los Angeles and India, but it was time to pick up the baggage once more, before midday prayer.

The attic room in the old part of the house was to be home to Tim for the next month. I couldn't help noticing that the bags contained papers and books. A holdall probably kept his clothes and washing gear, another carrier bag for shoes and his guitar case. But by far the greater part were the papers and books. I thought maybe there is a filing system here with the different coloured plastic bags, but to keep things safe in bags that are easily torn didn't make sense to me. I wanted to provide a suitcase that would keep it all tidy and secure. This is the way I like to work and I struggle watching others do differently. Tim asked if there was a telephone he could use to let folk know he had arrived and he pulled out an address book that in itself was falling to bits. I know my lists are many and not very well presented, but at least my contacts are safe. I needed to withdraw from Tim's chaos, so I hinted that Cyril would be in the garden if he wanted to wander around, and I said I would see him at midday prayer.

We hadn't really discussed what Tim would do at the friary while he was with us, as it all came about at short notice. General house duties would have to suffice to start with. The rest of the day went by quickly as the friary adjusted its new member. Tim found Cyril fascinating and seemed content to follow him round, listening intently to his stories. Cyril's face was alight as his stories poured out with newness. It had been a blustery day in more ways than one as the community headed towards evening prayer. Converging on the back door, I stood to one side and held it open as Tim clutched his guitar. As we walked towards the chapel, he looked at me and said "You seem to have the skill to be in the past, present and future, all at the same time. That's a gift". There wasn't time to reply as we stepped into the stillness of the chapel.

Thoughts of why Tim had brought his guitar to evening office and the bustle of the day left me. The wind had dropped quite quickly and the time of silence before office seemed to slow down to a gentle murmur. How could I be in the past, present and future? These sounded like prophetic words spoken into the now, and from such a young man. The silence calmed the mind and washed over my spirit, like drinking from a cool, fresh mountain stream. Spirit, the part that enables the rest of me, if I would but let it. Thoughts began to surround me as the planets orbit the sun, and I could see how many things in my life are centred on the past. Collection of family belongings, the importance of heritage, roots, shared beliefs. The future is my creative being, ideas of how to make things more understandable, enabling others to grow from the reality of the present to the possibilities of the future. This does all seem to interweave in a strange way. Acknowledging the past, present and future within the moment makes a lot of sense. I was beginning to wonder if Brother Timothy was a time traveller, when Brother Michael began prayers.

The reading was from Micah 4: *In the last days the mountain of the Lord's temple will be established as the highest of the mountains; it will be exalted above the hills, and peoples will stream to it. Many nations will come and say, "Come, let us go up to the mountain of the Lord, to the temple of the God of Jacob. He will teach us his ways, so that we may walk in his paths."*

Tim moved to the front with his guitar, struck a chord and suggested we either follow or just listen. He played finger style, which was gentle and flowing. The words were about the beauty of God and our worship to Him, and soon I was following this simple act of devotion. It was one of those moments I didn't want to end as Tim's words faded and just the guitar remained. There was no end, the notes just seemed to fade and Tim was left sitting there. The guitar was pointing to the ground and his right hand raised, palm up, as he said, "My Lord and my God, my Lord and my God." I needed to readjust my thoughts about Tim. He points in many challenging directions.

7 AMBROSE

The air felt thin that morning. There was little breeze and a quietness that amplified the sound of nature around us. As we busied ourselves with household chores, I felt I, too, should be quiet in my movement, so as not to disturb the atmosphere. My range of hearing was extended as I noticed the sound of a tractor. Only when I looked did I realise the true distance. I wondered how far this quietness was spread.

The letterbox has its own sound made up of clangs and rattles, since the spring no longer holds firm. As the post hit the hard floor, I could tell there was a great deal arriving that morning. My initial instinct was to rush to see what it was all about, but as the sound faded in my mind, so too did the urge to go. Break time was heralded by the sound of cups in the kitchen and as I arrived, the smell of fresh coffee greeted me. Michael had neatly laid out the post into groups of personal and business, Cyril had made some ginger biscuits that were laid cooling on the side. The quietness remained as little was said, just the sound of Michael tearing up circulars and saving envelopes for further use. My post was small and uninteresting, conferences I would be unlikely to attend and updates on education matters. I picked up one envelope and slipped it into my side pocket. It was from Rick, and I didn't want to open it just yet. The silence went on and I thought how we tend to cope better with chaos than quiet. We seemed lost for meaningful words or statements that would bring about conversation. Or maybe we were just enjoying the moment.

Often in the simplest of tasks, thoughts emerge that become challenges, ideas or solutions. Where do they come from? I know most of my best ideas for resources, teaching or preaching, tend to formulate early in the morning while shaving. Clearly nothing comes from nothing, so there must be a seed of thought, something that kicks it off. A word or phrase heard, an observation questioning – why does that happen that way? Listening to our mixture of emotions and wondering why they are knitted this way. There's a spiritual dimension, too, that seems external, yet personal at its core. If nothing comes from nothing, then our thoughts have purpose and shouldn't be disregarded as random nonsense. I would often immerse myself in the quiet, appearing to be deep in thought, expecting at any minute a revelation that would drive me forward. I am learning to continue with the practical and to be more aware of my thoughts, a little bit like solving a crossword puzzle.

There was time that day to walk, but not to just sit and dream. I headed to my special place and took with me a sketch pad. Now, I am not an artist by any stretch of the imagination, but I am confident in myself to accept that what I draw is just how it is. You know, if you don't compare your work with anything else, then it has to be just perfect. I very rarely show my sketches to anyone. Before long I had settled with my back up against an old tree. Looking into the woods with the path leading off to my right, the sun was glinting through the branches as they moved gently in the light breeze.

I pulled out Rick's letter and began to read. It was quite short, unusual for Rick, and I was all set to read of his adventures. Rick was convalescing following an accident, and I could sense in his writing it wasn't the injury that was bothering him, but the fact he was stuck at home. I resolved to write by return and share some of my recent travels. I knew how being housebound would be affecting him, we all take too much for granted, particularly our mobility.

I exchanged the letter for my sketch pad and began to pencil in the basic detail, completing the larger trees and curving path. I quickly filled in some of the thicket and then focused on one tree to the left and carefully drew some leaves larger and more detailed in the foreground. I paid more attention to the bark on this tree, too, whereas the rest of the picture was vaguer. I felt the picture was finished and held it at arm's length, with its reality beyond the image. Looking at the shading and pencil lines, there between the trees in the thicket, was what seemed like the outline of a figure; I checked back to the subject and nothing resembled that shape. Returning to the sketch I began to firm up the shape. It was in proportion to its surroundings and took the form of a man coming towards me. It was more than a little scary when I recognised him as my Good Samaritan.

It had been some time since I had given any thought to this character and I didn't want to get into a serious discussion about how tangible something must be to be part of reality. I was, however, content to allow my imagination to wander and pose some vague scenarios. He may have been a man of the road, a farm labourer, gardener or a wandering storyteller. Married or single, this must have been a local man. But what was his purpose and why am I meeting him now? I had already decided he was from the mid-1600s, I feel already introduced to this gentle man.

I am curious by nature and I love a mystery, but it has to be fathomed and understood so that I'm part of the story and can share it with others. The idea came to me quite simply, to write a short story about this man. By doing that, I would be able to create a solution and settle my mind. The alternative would be to never really rest, always wondering what had happened. It's very common for us to write a story around a situation to help us feel better about it. The world is flat, the world is round, both statements strongly defended at the time with stories that fit the statements. I could see how this man could have lived close by, here, where I was sitting, close by the river and with sufficient shelter.

Returning to the friary that afternoon, it was drawing cold and the walk back was to take just over an hour. I reached the road we call the Milly Mires, I have no idea why they call it that, I followed the road till it took me up to the moor top. Pewits were performing their aerobatics, while sheep were moving towards lower ground. I pulled up my hood as the first drops of rain fell. I remember thinking, one of two things could happen here. Either I was going to get very wet, or some kind soul would offer me a lift. As the shortest route was by footpath through the moor, the former was to be true.

It was during that walk home, probably to take my mind off the weather, that the story of Ambrose, (my Good Samaritan), began to take shape. The name Ambrose appears twice in my family tree and I felt I wanted more of a close link with this character. He had indeed lived through the religious difficulties of Catholic persecution, studied and taken Holy Orders. Supported by recusants of this area, he had been successful in avoiding the authorities for over two years. I pictured a number of hiding places where this young man would have taken refuge and began to imagine how this lifestyle might have affected his sense of wellbeing. The stresses of my simple life were nothing compared to living in fear of capture, imprisonment and more than likely, death. My story was clearly following a similar line to Nicholas Postgate. Hearing those stories as a boy had given me a sense of danger and excitement around the Church, very different to what I experienced on a Sunday morning. My mind raced as I filled in details of secret marriages, close escapes and taking Holy Communion to the sick and dying. On a practical issue, I struggled to imagine how Ambrose managed to know where to be and when – how would people contact him? Under these conditions, Ambrose and many like him were unable to live out their values and beliefs in the real world, appearing to conform to the statutes of the land.

I was totally wet through as I reached the friary and headed straight to the bathroom. That evening I wrote up the story so far. Ambrose became more of a real person as I described colour, sound and emotion to the content of this tale.

We came together for the final office of the day, (Compline). Normal order was resumed. Each busy thought, each wild imagining fell away in the silence of the chapel. There was not a breath of wind to disturb the trees and I stayed a while after the others had gone. A candle flame was frozen in the stillness and its bands of coloured light held me in awe of its beauty. I would normally associate the words flicker and flame to candles. Within this stillness I knew, I must return to who I was before the fall and these recent wanderings. There was much to be getting on with and the comfort of the routine would settle my spirit, too. I felt I wanted to do something, and stepping to the altar, laid face down as I did when I took my vows. I stayed there only a moment, then got up, blew out the candles and left for bed.

8 BEING THE SAME BUT DIFFERENT

Michael would normally attend meetings of our Order, but this time he suggested I went instead. The meeting was to be at our house in Aylesbury, some 240 miles away. Michael had already booked the train ticket for me. Planned out like a military operation and listed in detail, Michael was to drive me to York, keeping the journey to two changes. York to London Kings Cross, then Marylebone to Aylesbury, it seemed straightforward but the bit in the middle was more concerning for me. I was not at all familiar with the underground system. I noticed I was due into Kings Cross at seven minutes past nine and to leave Marylebone at twelve minutes past ten. The instructions for the underground read, "From Kings Cross St Pancras Underground Station take the Hammersmith & City Line or the Circle Line (Westbound, Platform 1) to Baker Street Underground Station, from Baker Street walk to London Marylebone (approximately 10 minutes)." When I plan, I like to build in a measure of time that will cope with delays or wrong turns, even if I end up early at my destination. This nervous feeling inside was familiar and I remembered in my school days, the instructor pushing me on to swim a width of the pool. I held my breath and with long breaststrokes, keeping my head out of the water, didn't let go till I reached the other side. I found a strategy of metaphorically holding my breath, until I did, what I didn't want to do. Often, of course, I would just avoid the activity if at all possible. This trip to Aylesbury was not something I could avoid, and so many people manage trains every day. I had to imagine myself on an adventure.

It was during morning coffee that I remembered Rick lived in Launton, just outside Bicester, a stone's throw from Aylesbury. I decided there and then to call him and see if we could meet up. It had been difficult keeping up with correspondence, as Rick was always on the move – bit of a one way conversation, really. I hunted through my desk for Rick's business card and called his mobile number. "David, how are you?" It was Rick I was concerned for, and not wanting to get into a long conversation, I quickly mentioned my meeting in Aylesbury. He insisted I took a day out and visited him. There was a bus from Aylesbury to Bicester, passing through Launton that would drop me off at the pub. Rick's house was only fifty yards before the stop. That seemed simple enough and a conversation with Michael confirmed that my trip to Aylesbury was to be extended by twenty four hours.

The evening before, I began to pack a small suitcase. I recalled Brother Timothy, who had only stayed with us in the end for four weeks, but seemed to move around the world effortlessly and with a great deal of luggage. I was caught between taking essentials and all those extras to occupy my time on the journey. I opted for just a notebook and pen – this could be an opportunity to write some more. Sometimes I'm amazed at the countless things that go through my mind before making a decision. I'm sure time spent processing these thoughts would be better spent in other areas. It's just the way I am and I always say I am no different to anyone else.

There was still a mist in the dales that morning, as we drove over the moor top towards York. Michael was still going through the journey plan, making sure I hadn't forgotten anything, and I was telling myself for the umpteenth time, everything was going to be all right. I appreciated Michael's support but didn't expect to be escorted all the way onto the platform, Michael taking on the role of parent, seeing the child off to boarding school. There was a feeling of déjà vu as my mother would have the same need to make sure all was just as it should be. It's a strong emotion, this paradox of wanting to do everything myself, and preferring others to do much of it; wanting perfection and settling for much less.

This idea of paradox was to follow me as I found a seat and settled into the first part of my journey. I had managed to be in a seat immediately surrounded by empty seats; as much as I like people around me, I prefer my own company. My paradoxical thoughts continued as examples came to mind; the Ship of Theseus. Theseus' ship returned from Crete and was preserved by the Athenians. Decaying timbers were replaced and the question asked was whether it was still Theseus' ship. In The Wizard of Oz, the woodcutter tin man, whose axe was enchanted by the witch, cut off a limb and was replaced with a prosthetic. Over time this poor woodcutter became a tin man, but the tinsmith who helped him neglected to replace his heart. Was this tin man or wood cutter?

I was no longer the young man I used to be. Now with a full beard and much larger round the middle. On the inside, a different perspective of what was going on. At what point did this young man become someone else, or is he still residing within this shell? The paradox, as to which side is right can only serve as a thought exercise to prove that both sides can be right without conflict. I was counselling a young man once and reached a point where he said, "I'm nobody" I knew we had made progress, as we cannot hold this statement. If I am, then I must be, therefore I cannot be nobody. That young man went on to discover himself and begin to value who he was. By this point of my journey, I was beginning to wonder who I was!

I still hadn't put pen to paper regarding the story of Ambrose and decided to stretch my legs and get a cup of coffee. I was fascinated by the buzz of conversation and mixture of colours and poses, as folk dealt with the process of travelling, each one different but at this point of their journey, together on this train. Returning to my seat, I eased back and felt I could just rest my eyes. I was disturbed by a voice asking if he could speak to me. It was a young man, I would guess mid-twenties. My garments were a bit of a giveaway as to my occupation. He asked what Order I was and if he could sit for a while. I didn't bargain for a travelling companion, but it's difficult to say no. His name was Simon and he'd just finished a degree in Social History. He was on his way to London to look at some job prospects. I had wondered what would be a career path after a Social History degree. He told me he was pursuing accountancy and banking. This was a young man who seemed to have a map of where he was going and was carefully picking out the most direct route. We talked around many subjects that revealed a caring person, pleasant and full of options – a refreshing contrast to the gloom portrayed by our media. I didn't see his next question coming – how do you know if you have a vocation to the priesthood? I told him that was probably one of the most difficult questions, as there are as many answers as there are people who ask it. Simon went on at length to tell me about his attraction towards becoming a priest, his involvement at his local church and the chaplaincy at the university. I wanted to tell him my story, of how I had become a friar and why I thought I was there. I felt my own passion rise; I took a breath and held it. This was not the time to talk about me, I could see Simon had a calling that needed to be explored further. I was surprised he had kept it hidden so long and not spoken to anyone about it. I suggested he spoke to his own priest and that doors would either open or close for him. We talked for another fifteen minutes or so and he may have sensed my tiredness, as he then returned to his own seat.

With eyes closed but not asleep, I began to review the story of Ambrose. I was quite clear about where he had come from and what he was about. His values and beliefs were solid and his determination to maintain his way of life seemed without question. I had imagined Ambrose aged in his mid-forties. He would labour in the fields to earn just enough to keep him. Ambrose was a contemplative and spent much time in quiet prayer and thought. He was very much isolated from other priests, as the structure of the church was in hiding. The Roman Catholics of England were known as recusants, from the Latin word to reject, refusing to accept or obey the established authority. I had to admit I was now stuck. I had created this person, who was woven into this secret world, his strength coming from a mystical source although firmly rooted in the practical service of his flock. I had entered into the reality of Ambrose, I could smell the woodland and hear the river. But where to next? What will become of this simple, holy man?.

9 LEARNING A LITTLE MAGIC

My bags were already in my hand as the train reached its final station. I stepped onto the platform and into a sea of people. This old building was amazing. If only I had time to take it all in. Our railway system is something to be marvelled at. Originating in the 1800s, for the most part it runs on time. The other amazing thing is that no one person runs the system.

I had rehearsed Michael's instructions and, picking up speed, made my way to Marylebone Station. The whole pace of life here was noticeably faster and getting from A to B seeming more of an inconvenience of time for people. The journey was much better than I expected.

Arrival at the house was brief as I entered into the buzz. The Order seemed to be a mix of connections and catch-ups, not something I do well. I found myself a chair and sat down with pen and paper as the proceedings began. I was on edge not to miss anything, as Michael would want a full report. This was out of my comfort zone, the security of the old friary, spending most of my time in the doing of things and leaving the planning to those who plan. The gap between these two (planning and doing) was shrinking fast. My interest level was picking up and I found myself beginning to see the importance of understanding both. My words, brief as they were, focused on relationships and clear communication. We so often talk without considering the why, or the action that provides the outcome we strive for.

Socialising that evening became easier as common language filled the air. Laughter and reminiscing, debating the future, as we grow and respond to change. I was ready to retire an hour before I managed to steal away to bed. My body felt as if it was still going at the speed of the train. The young man came to mind as I wondered which path he would choose. I had no conscious sense of what would enter my thoughts or the direction of them. As if running through fast-forward, the video skipped scenes until quite abruptly it stopped. And there was Ambrose. A stillness fell and it must have been shortly after that I entered sleep.

Early morning prayer with the brothers, familiar words sung in a different place; this had the effect of calming the soul and reassuring the mind. I spent the next two hours tending to the practical aspects of my visit, making sure I had collected everything Michael would expect. A Brother Bernard took my hand and expressly asked him to be remembered to Cyril. I felt awkward about leaving early, but excited about this part of my journey.

The bus between Aylesbury and Launton took just over the hour, following the timetable and Rick's directions from The Bull. The door was part open and he called me in as I knocked. Rick explained how folk from the village had been popping in to check if he needed anything. I asked if there was a rota but he said no it just happens – he had no idea how. I busied myself in the kitchen, preparing some lunch with things I'd brought with me while Rick began to tell me tales of his adventures. I was beginning to see just how much we had in common. My adventures were internal imaginings, whereas Rick had done the miles. It is possible, I thought, to go many miles without discovering anything. Over lunch, I listened more to Rick's language than the detail of his conversation, understanding more of the person. What would he make of Ambrose?

I had begun to wonder, to what degree had I become consumed with Ambrose and for what purpose? It was when I began to speak about him that I felt as if I was losing my marbles.

Rick was quite philosophical about his injury. It had caused him to stop and consider what next: advancing years, fitness, health and general wellbeing; there was need of a plan. Rick was to use his skills and experience as a consultant, based at home and travelling only in the UK. His passion, I learnt, was to paint and an old shed down the garden, would be converted into a studio. This all sounded just perfect. I had to confess to myself a small amount of envy. I could never see myself as an artist but to find the time to do something like that, was very attractive!

The house was immaculate and ordered, full of interesting items, but not on show like a museum, part of the structure and fitting together like a kettle and a stove. Rick wanted to hear all about the friary, its occupants and visitors, and soon I got round to speaking about Ambrose. The whole story came out and I waited for an explanation. Surely Rick had thoughts on this kind of thing, having travelled far and wide? I went on till I got to the point in my story when I can't seem to get any further. It was then that it dawned on me that I had to decide on an ending before I could go any further. It was as if I was waiting for someone to tell me how it ends. How could I presume to know what happens to Ambrose? Rick just smiled and said reality is what we create.

Rick began to tell part of his own story. He had written it down some time ago and entitled it Hiding Place –

I've always loved hiding places, being of small build I could often get into places others couldn't even imagine. During a game of hide and seek, the seeker could be looking right at me; it was as if I were invisible. I had climbed into another world through that very small gap in reality. It really didn't matter where I was, I could always find an entrance; under or behind, through or above, it was all the same to me. I had a fascination for doorways, the smaller the better and in the most unusual places; to find a way from one place to another by a route not yet explored was my mission.

Hiding places were my genius. There were two challenges; one to find the ultimate hide and two, the challenge for them to find me. Often, when it was safe, I would run from hide to hide; the risk of being seen was high but it was so exciting, I could burst. Being the seeker was not as much fun, it was not difficult to find them. I would call out to make them laugh and give away their cover; the run back to base was swift as I ran with determination not to be beaten. In this arena I could excel with ingenuity and creative prowess; they had to do the work, to discover me! Hiding was a skill that became a strategy, to hide myself in this other world, to become invisible to those outside.

It was not even during a game; I was walking through the local woods and I saw what looked like an entrance within the dense shrubs within seconds I was lost in a magical world. The sounds of nature were amplified, drowning out any sense of people and people's busyness. The way the branches knitted together brought shapes and colours to my imagination and I became one with this new world. It was as if I had fallen asleep but I knew I was wide awake; I was watching the branches grow, which sounds ridiculous now, but that was exactly what was happening. This was an excellent hiding place and I visited it often, just to be there.

Life brings responsibility and the hiding place became a distant memory. My strategy of being invisible took on many different roles and the search for hiding places never left me. That magical world was so inviting, but for practical reasons, I was bound to this world. Until one day I realised, I had to be present in both worlds at the same time; this would signify emerging from my hiding place, and becoming fully visible.

As Rick read aloud his story, I was amid my woodlands in North Yorkshire, blending in to the natural world, while entering another dimension. "Before you go, I want to give you something," Rick said, and opening a drawer he pulled out a small box. "I found it in an old bazaar, I am sure it is not as old as it looks" and he laughed. "It's very simple magic but when performed well, is very convincing." There was a silk handkerchief and what seemed to be an egg. Rick expertly made the egg vanish and then reappear in the box. I was impressed. The illusion was disclosed and following a little practice, I managed to master this new art.

Being tied to the return bus, I bade Rick goodbye, with a promise of hospitality at the friary upon his recovery. This was agreed and before long I was collecting my other belongings from Aylesbury. The return journey to York seemed quicker, as I busied myself writing notes concerning how Ambrose would complete his journey.

BROTHER DAVID

10 A SKYLARK AND A SQUIRREL

Ambrose had never lost faith in being who he was. His service to others would always be found. Neither was he ever discovered by those who would take his life to the edge. An opportunity arose within a family that enabled him to stay with them, taking on another identity, worshiping in both the established church and in the old ways. Ambrose passed away under a different name and no trace would ever be found. He was buried in the family space and rests eternal.

Faith is eternal and is evident in the living, perpetuated through death, carried on a wind and grasped by many. Faith has shape and form, dependant on how it is held and shared. I didn't feel a need to continue in the quest for Ambrose, nor to delve into family records. His legacy is our faith.

Michael was waiting – it's good to have predictable folk around you. He must have sensed my tiredness, as conversation was limited. I'm sure I dozed off as we passed the rigg. Just 25 minutes and I would be able to unload at the friary. Great excursions are really not my thing. The old wooden door to the tractor shed had been left open as we pulled straight in. Cyril came out to greet me. You would have thought I'd been to the ends of the earth. Supper was already prepared and I began to share all about Aylesbury. I remembered Brother Bernard to Cyril, his memory was sharp as his face lit up and he accounted where and when they last served together. Michael seemed pleased with my reporting and I think I felt a little pleased with myself too. Michael asked how my visit to Rick had gone and I was tempted to reveal the magic box, but decided to wait for another day. Magic is meant for special moments and it's more about recognising that moment than performing the illusion.

It must have been over four weeks later. I was overdue a walk and the call back to the woodlands above the river was strong. It was a fine day with little wind, and I took nothing with me apart from my thoughts. In many ways my woodland sanctuary is where my journey began, although it was later that I became aware I had been journeying many years. This place had become so intimate that I didn't need to physically be there to experience the peace. I was hoping the visit would enable pieces to fit together. My path thus far had many diversions, although a sense of purpose was to be found in much of the detail. Was this a time to move on from the friary? I felt on the edge of something different.

I was attracted by the song of a skylark and as I turned I noticed an old farmer leaning over a wall and drawing on his pipe. "Now then" – a typical Yorkshire greeting. I responded, "Aye, not a bad day." He was taking a break from repairing a dry stone wall, his flat cap perched on the back of his head, in no way covering a mop of straggly greying hair. He lifted the bottle top off his pipe and struck another match. We spoke for a few moments and then conversation got round to the skylark. He told me this was the minstrel of the air and that if I listened carefully I would hear three stages. Rising to the heavens, full of energy and excitement of its destination, fully motivated; nothing is going to stop it. Reaching his zenith, the song becomes more of a proclamation of identity; this is who I am and what I am about. Returning to the ground, his song slows a little, not surprisingly as this small bird has sung his heart out. I had often heard this song, but only then did I pick out the stages and sense the changes within.

Leaving the farmer behind, I travelled on, towards the woods and my sitting place. I dwelled on the skylark, I have known this bird all my life. He has become a personal friend, along with the curlew and pewit. These birds have not changed in their song or aerial acrobatics. They could easily be the same birds as in the days of Ambrose.

There was a pull on my legs as I reached the top and rested for a moment at the wishing stone. Another fifty or so yards and I sat down and listened to the gentle sounds. I began also to listen to my thoughts, wanting so much to put them in an order I could work with. There was so much, I decided to create a very large sheet of paper in my mind. What was important to me? My community of brothers, even those in Aylesbury and beyond. Friendships: such as Rick, local folk and how that builds a picture. My routine of prayer: work, study and rest. The Franciscan Rule that gives me the structure and guidance and my belief that in all this, I have freedom to choose. My greatest value today as I sit here, is who I am. I don't think that would have been on my sheet before. I went on to list many more things I valued and that form my beliefs. This process was magic in its nature, which got me thinking about my new skill and the disappearing egg.

If I were to go through the motions of performing magic, to vanish an egg and make it reappear would certainly do just that. But if I were to believe in magic (even though I knew it was an illusion), then the effect would be mesmerising. The purpose of magic is to show that the impossible is possible.

Most people watch the illusion and are amazed how their eyes are deceived and their mind tells them they have just witnessed the impossible. Rational thought takes over and the inevitable question, "How is it done?" There is a force greater than magic at work here, between wanting to know and not wanting to know. The fact that you know it's an illusion is enough. If we take away the magic, it's quite possible we'll lose the ability to achieve the impossible.

What is my magic, how am I meant to use it and where? Although this was not something I could answer, I had lots of reasons in my mind. Why I was not where I could be? There seemed so much of it: my parents, school, the Church. I began to see it all and it was mind-confusing. My preferred time for this would be in the chapel and a long conversation with God. The weight was too much, it would take forever to speak of it. If only there were a way to plug in and download everything. That's what I wanted to happen, with all my heart that was my desire.

It began with a sense of trusting as each and every thought left me. The whole process took only a few moments and left me in a heightened sense of awareness; valued. Then the strangest thing happened. A small squirrel came up and sat next to me. He came from behind but I saw it all without turning my head. He sat within touching distance. We both sat there gazing out into the aether. I was seeing the world in a very different way, full of opportunities, and I was sharing this moment with one of the smallest creatures of this habitat. There was a second when our eyes met before he scampered off into the thicket.

Now, I could go on to tell this story many times, and folk would be amazed. But if that were to be, then it might as well never happened. For everything has a purpose and this was for me to take forward. This was an open door and over this threshold, things would be different.

The next half-hour found me whittling at a stick. I was taking off the rough end and fashioning a knuckle that would sit in the palm of my hand. I had a walking stick back at the friary, but this one would be cut to my size. The walk back was brisk as new thoughts arrived.

11 EVERY INCH A BRIDGE

Cyril and I were making breakfast. He had designs on cereal and toast, I was preparing a full English for myself. The whole process was going on amid the absence of speech. There was a complete awareness of where Cyril needed to be in his preparations and my movements were not restricting his. It was the silence I noticed, not the movement.

Cyril broke the silence with words that sounded as if he had been thinking them for some time. "It will be the same if you go or if you stay." Not a question that required an answer and I was stunned into not knowing what to say. The silence continued. I had never spoken, I don't think, or even thought about leaving. Should I just dismiss the remark as Cyril's ramblings?

I sat at the table, took a moment to give thanks and began to eat. I asked Cyril what made him think I was leaving. We all want to leave, he said; it's what keeps us here. Was there something in the way I had been that implies I want to move on, that I was unsettled. My mind raced through all I could remember, I didn't want it to appear that I wasn't pulling my weight.

There came a knock at the door. I was only half way through my breakfast and the vow of obedience doesn't come easy even with time. It was a parcel delivery for me, but I didn't know anyone in the United

States, and I certainly wasn't expecting a parcel. The item was about the size of a shoe box. I placed it on the dresser and returned to my breakfast. "Are you not going to open it?" Cyril asked. I was determined to finish my breakfast while it was hot. The package had been in transit for some time, it could wait a little longer.

I am sure Cyril was more interested in the contents of the parcel than I was. He suggested clearing the table while I opened it. Carefully wrapped, the box was not heavy and did not rattle. The small sender's label removed the mystery. It was Brother Timothy who went to Los Angeles and had been visiting San Francisco. The item was well packed, wrapped in newspaper and cardboard. A jug with the Yorkshire white rose and the words, City of York. A simple message saying he had found it in a church sale and thought of me and how perhaps it was time to send it home. Well! What was I to do with what I guess was a milk jug? He should have sold it there and then, probably would have got a few dollars for it. It certainly cost more to post it here. What on earth was he thinking of and why would he imagine I would like it? I didn't think I was a milk jug person. To me, the only place this would look right would be in a bric-a-brac shop.

I began to wonder what it was that Timothy had seen in me, that caused him to visualise me – who did he think I was! Timothy only met me for a short period of time and his disorganisation really aggravated me. However, on both sides of this table, I could see things that betray who I was.

I had left the box and packaging in the hall, thinking at least that would come in handy, but then headed with it to the recycling bin. Separating the paper from the cardboard, I noticed a postcard. It was the San Francisco's Golden Bridge, perhaps the only postcard to be found there. On the back of the card, a few words were written:

"David, you are every inch a bridge, stretching out to both sides. You have an ability to understand and convey simply to others. The jug declares its identity, whilst having a very practical purpose. I am doing fine – PAX Tim."

The component parts went into the relevant recycling boxes and I slipped the postcard into my tunic. I had some preparation work to complete for a school project and decided to spend some time in the library. This room is like an old friend that just accepts me, warts and all. I can breathe deeper sighs, it makes no judgements about me and I can return to a more balanced state.

On one level, the task was progressing well and on the other, my inner self was processing identity. My status seemed to be. The more I knew me, the more likely people will see who I am. I was busy uncovering something complex and using simple language, enabling others to understand, and there was a hint of excitement as I engaged fully in my central purpose.

Midday prayer brought us two visitors, a young couple, I guess in their thirties, married with no children as yet. They seemed keen to ask questions, searching to find their place. Their devotion and worship was fresh and uplifting and it was as if their need to be part of ministry, was printed on their T-shirts in big letters. The Church is in desperate need of workers such as these. I wanted to tell them to go away, find themselves, and together they would find their right path. This was not what they wanted to hear, so I did not tell them. The couple were gifted with music and at the slightest opportunity, a guitar would appear. We spoke about love and how without love in the equation, the outcome would not appear quite right. This couple were to visit the friary often over the next few years. It was good to see the shift, as they moved away from their busyness and followed their hearts' calling. A path emerged for them, albeit vague for most of the time. Their commitment and love enabled them to move forward, even when, at times, the path had seemed so obscure. Their music became a way in which they spent time, sharing themselves with folk.

Today in the library I am writing again, for in a journey, there is always "just a little farther." We have an understanding, this chair and I. It has to be in the library, where all things come together. Here, magic can take place. Appearing and disappearing, transformations are enabled through a belief in possibilities; by putting aside the false beliefs and allowing me to take shape.

I feel as if my journey has just begun, and that my time spent thus far has been chasing many paths. I have learnt that magic is possible in other places, and not just my chair in the library.

BROTHER DAVID

12 EPILOGUE

It has been almost seven years now since Ambrose and my walks in Arncliffe woods. I have arrived at a place very different, and this chair, though practical, is not as comfortable as the last one. Looking through my journals, names appear and I wonder where they are now. Brother Michael, still the practical and organised one is still leading the work at the old friary – with a new, young friar, Brother Andrew. Dear Brother Cyril, passed away in his sleep just three years ago. We discovered that Cyril had never been his real name, but that it had adopted him in his college years, and he decided to stay with it. His wise words and strange phrases will go on with me.

Mrs Johnson, although hardly mentioned, was the least seen around the friary, but an essential part of that small community, enabling the brothers to do what they do. I can speak of Mrs Johnson, as she would never under any circumstances do so herself. Her quietness in all she did was remarkable, and she often knew where we have left our lost items. It all seems so far away now.

Letters arrive and depart every six to eight weeks between Rick and me. It is strange in this day and age to use the paper rather than email. The words convey much more, as the handwriting shifts in size and weight. I did manage to create a Blog site, which was great fun. Rick is talking about a visit in the fall. Other characters that come to mind, Harry for example. They enter our lives, often leave a mark and then exit. Such meetings always have purpose and we should ask ourselves, "What is my learning?"

A LONG JOURNEY HOME

It was an ordinary day at the friary, Brother Michael came to me in the library. "There's going to be some changes" he said. "The Order is asking you to move on" he continued. Always brief and to the point, Michael seems to lack emotion, but I know this is not the case. This new journey was awaiting my decision, but I got the impression I was expected to say yes. I thought things were mapped out for me, and that things would continue as they were. To uproot from North Yorkshire was probably going to be the hardest thing I had ever done, and the time-scale was short. Leaving behind belongings that did not belong, projects and resources that would not be needed. The needs and resources in our world are becoming further apart and the Franciscan call to the poor, homeless and marginalised is our mission. I flew out to California, to meet Brother Tim in Los Angeles, and there to serve those in most need, with the basics; food, shelter and listening.

My transition came with much internal conflict, having been relatively content, in the security of the friary, and the familiarity of my surroundings. Effecting a real escape into solitude and reflection, how was this going to work? Where would I find my Skylark? What sense did it make, to switch serving roles at this stage of the game?

It was Brother Tim's turn to meet me at the railway station, following the longest journey of my life. I felt exhausted and welcomed the help with my few belongings. The first two days were a blur, but on the third morning I went to morning Mass. Some of the people who used the centre, the homeless and the poor were there. At communion I watched as they came to receive. It was as if God were saying, "These are my people" and tears began to flow. I pondered on my long journey, and realised I was always close to my destination.

Ambrose will always remain on the edge of reality, between our waking and sleeping. Folk such as Ambrose are guides along our journey, becoming more visible as the mist clears.

To share is to grow

Pax et bonum
David.

BROTHER DAVID

ABOUT THE AUTHOR

A Yorkshire man, in love with the moors and writing his fist small novel. He has been telling stories for many a year, being brought up in this tradition – and finds a way to make them relevant to our everyday life. It seems there is much we can learn about ourselves, when we reflect on things gone by.

The writing of the book was a journey in itself, taking longer than expected, but perhaps that was the way it needed to be. As Brother David remarked; "We need an ending, to see where we are going."

BROTHER DAVID